© Aladdin Books Ltd

Designed and produced by
Aladdin Books Ltd
70 Old Compton Street
London W1

ISBN 0-531-04658-3

Separation by La Cromolito, Milan

Printed in Belgium

First published in
the United States in 1983 by
Franklin Watts,
387 Park Avenue South,
New York, NY 10016.

Contents

MAKE IT YOURSELF

Christmas

Consultant Caroline Pitcher

Illustrated by Louise Nevett

Franklin Watts

New York · London · Toronto · Sydney

About this book

The projects in this book are designed for children to make by themselves or with a group of friends. Children can follow the sequence of instructions through pictures, whether or not they can read. The text is included for the parent/teacher to give additional hints and tips.

The "What you need" panel shows clearly what is required for each project. No supervision is required – except where this symbol appears ⚠.

The materials needed for the projects are usually available in most homes or classrooms. Where certain materials may not be available, alternatives are given. It is a good idea to collect all sorts of household bits and pieces. See Page 30.

The level of difficulty of the projects varies slightly to cater to children of differing abilities.

 Where this symbol appears, adult help is required. Look for it.

Cutting
Children should never be given sharp knives or scissors, and for most projects in this book they are unnecessary. There are many types of children's scissors available with rounded ends. Where objects are difficult to cut – for example, potatoes or plastic dish-washing liquid bottles – an adult should supervise. These instances are marked with the danger symbol. Where a plastic bottle is specified, be sure that it does not contain any dangerous liquids such as bleach or disinfectant. Always rinse out bottles, whatever they have contained.

Gluing
Any sort of paste or glue is suitable for making most of the projects, but in certain cases a strong glue is required and this is illustrated with a red asterisk on the glue pot. An adult should supervise when strong glue is being used.

Coloring
Most projects can be successfully colored with powder paint or ordinary watercolor. For shiny or plastic surfaces use poster paint, powder paint, or tempura paint mixed with a PVA medium. Look for the AP or CP seal of approval. Where projects are to be used in water, use wax crayons to color them.

Powder paint, poster paint, and wax crayons are all nontoxic and lead-free. Alternative coloring methods are colored pencils (crayons), or felt-tip pens and pastels. Ensure that the felt-tips you use are nontoxic.

One of the simplest ways of applying color is to cut out the required shape from colored paper and glue it onto the project.

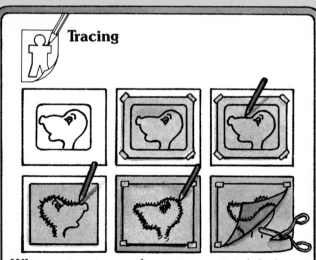

Tracing

Where a tracing outline appears it is labeled with the tracing symbol. Tape the tracing paper over the outline. Trace the outline. Turn over the tracing and rub a pencil thickly on the back. Tape the tracing, outline upward, on paper or cardboard, and retrace the outline.

What you need:

What the symbols mean

Glue

Strong glue

Scissors

Paint

Kitchen knife

Pencil

Paintbrush

Fat felt-tip pen

Thin felt-tip pen

Wax crayon

Paper

Thin cardboard

Thick cardboard

Tracing paper

Tinfoil

Pipe cleaner

Rubber band

Toothpicks

Drinking straw

Modeling clay

String

Yogurt or cream container

Coin

Cork

Cotton thread spool

Popsicle stick

Bottle cap

Small cardboard roll

Matchbox lid

Matchbox tray

Used matchsticks

Scotch tape

Small box

Dish-washing liquid bottle

Knitting yarn

Milk or juice carton

Large box

Santa Claus

- If you do not have a cardboard tube you can make one with a sheet of cardboard, rolled and glued together.

- Trace the outline in picture 18 onto cardboard to make the arms, and glue them into position.

- Make a sack for Santa Claus using brown paper, folded and glued along the sides, or stitch a piece of brown cloth.

- Stuff the sack with cotton and tuck it under Santa's hands.

What you need:

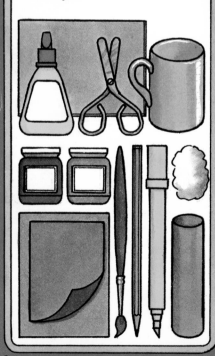

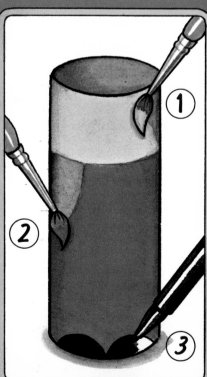

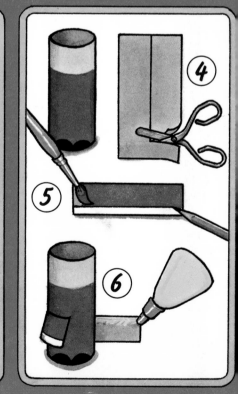

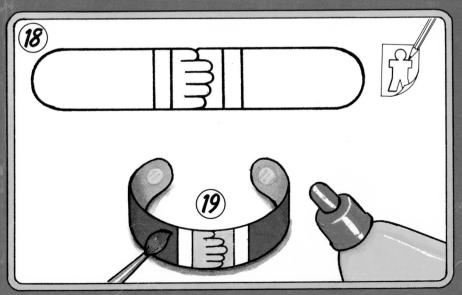

Reindeer and Sleigh

- Trace the outline of the runner twice and of the reindeer's body once.

- The tray from a large matchbox is best for the sleigh, but any box of similar size will work.

- The heavy lines of the reindeer show where to cut, the dotted line where to fold.

What you need:

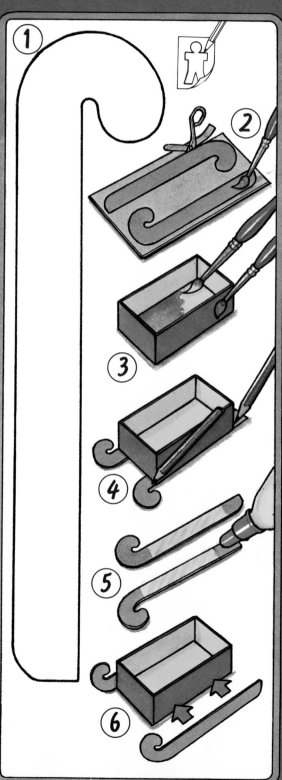

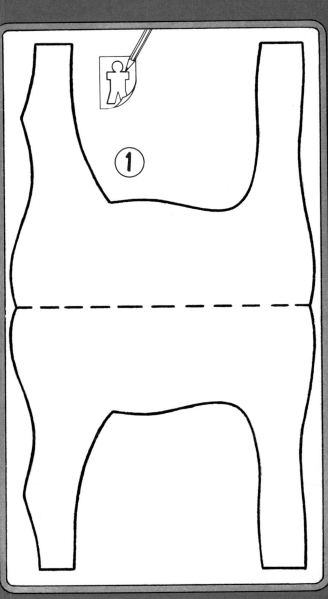

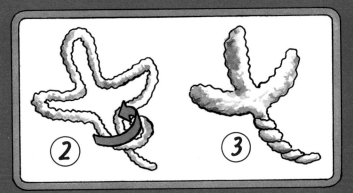

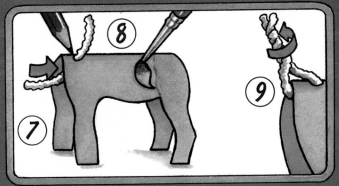

Paper Garlands

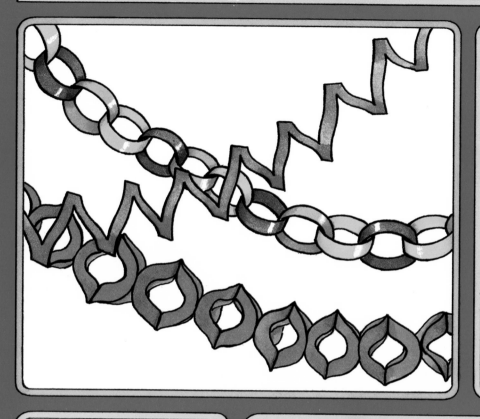

- Use any sort of colored paper to make these garlands – even patterned wrapping paper will do.

- For the third garland, make lots of circles from the tracing outline. Or you can draw around a teacup for the outer ring and an eggcup for the inner ring to make a bigger garland.

- If you have no colored paper, paint lots of plain paper in bright colors before you start.

What you need:

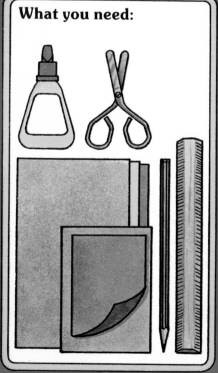

① ② ③ ④

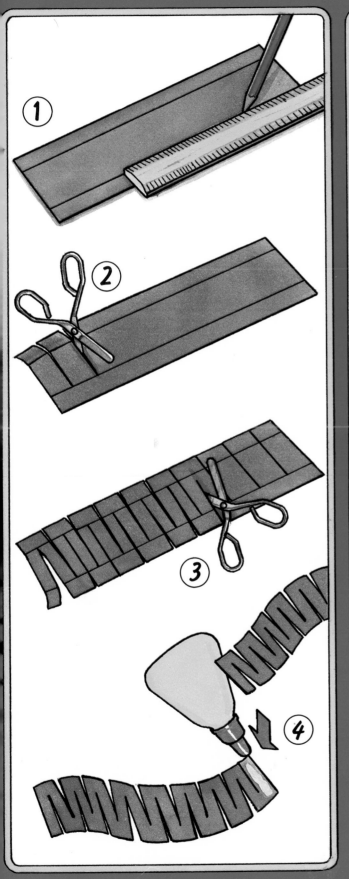

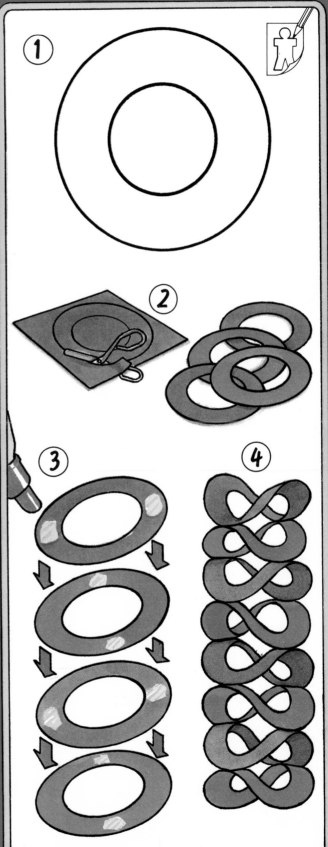

Tree Decorations

- Trace the star outline onto cardboard. If you do not have a pipe cleaner, you can hang the decoration with string or thread.

- Paint any design onto cardboard to make the lantern.

- When making the Christmas ball, be sure to attach the pipe cleaner (or thread secured with a knot) before gluing together the two halves.

What you need:

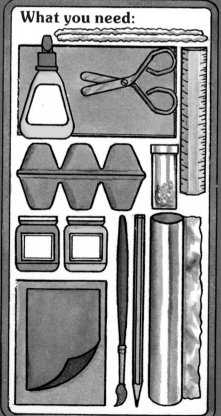

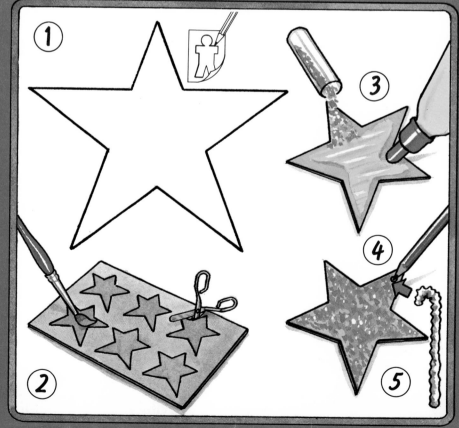

1
2
3
4
5

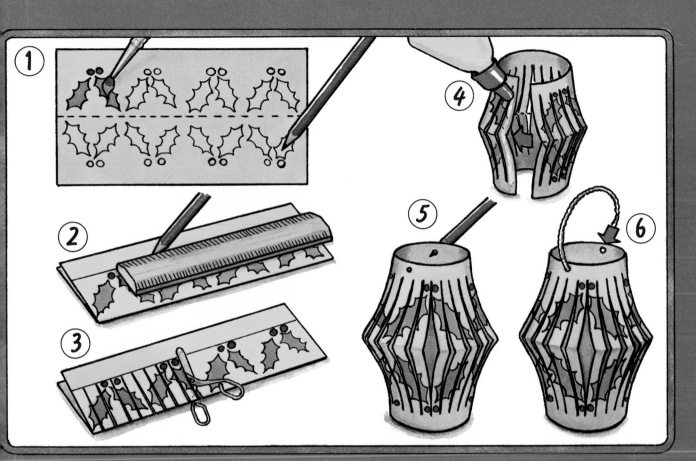

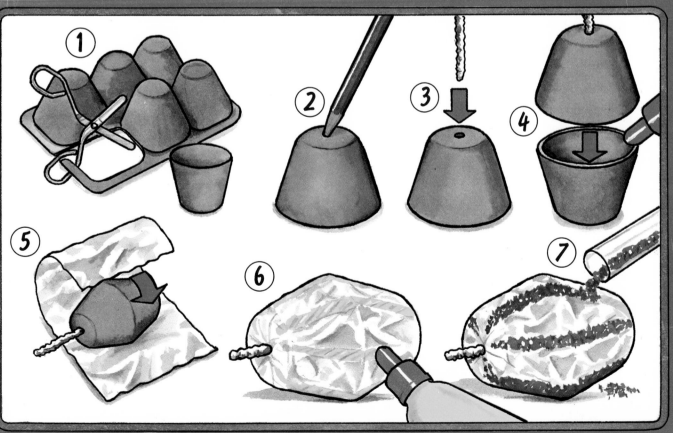

Snowman

- Trace the outline in picture 9 to make the brim for the hat, or draw around an eggcup.

- Any sort of bottle top will work for the top of the hat. Or mold modeling clay into shape and paint the brim in the same color.

- Use buttons, beads, or painted pieces of paper to decorate the snowman.

- You can use a twig for the walking stick if you do not have a pipe cleaner.

What you need:

① ②

③

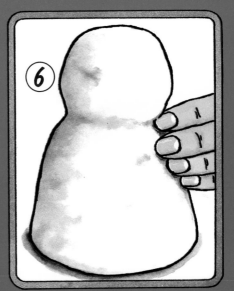

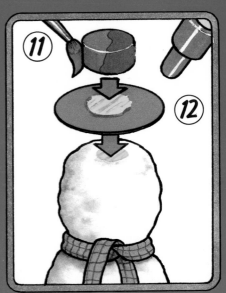

Christmas Cards

- Paint decorations on the outside of the Christmas tree card and write your message inside.

- Trace the outline of the angel card. The solid lines show where you cut, the dotted lines show where you fold. Press the scissors through the card and cut only around the solid lines of the angel.

- Trace the hexagon shape three times onto a card, arranged as shown.

What you need:

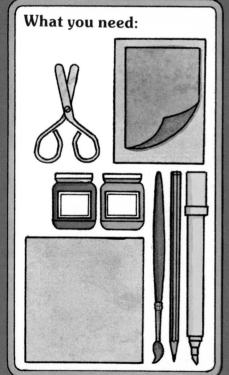

① ② ③ ④

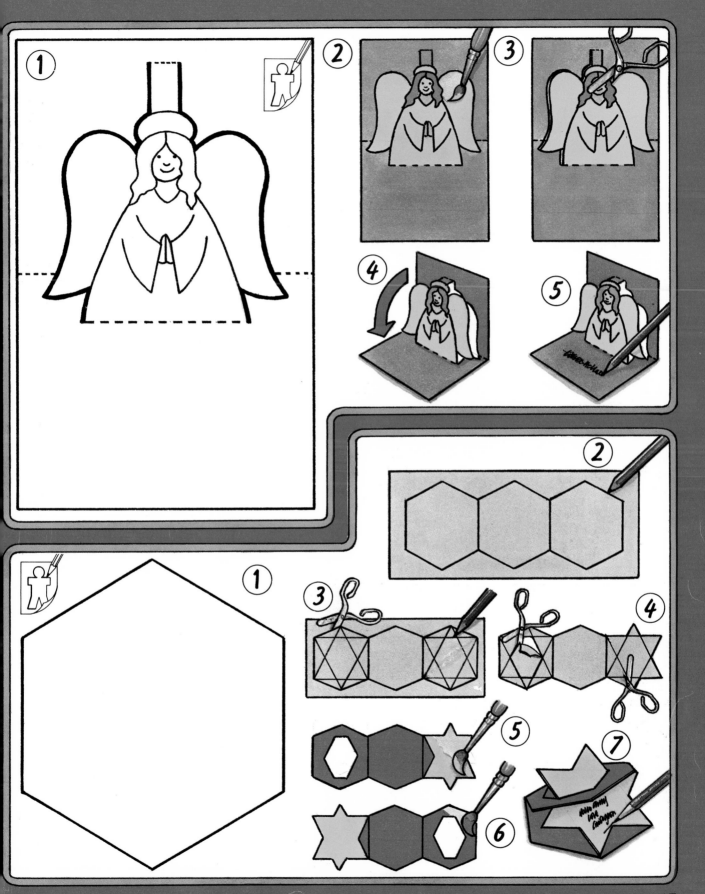

Christmas Tree

- Trace the outline in picture 1 onto paper and paint it.

- Trace the outline in picture 7 onto four sheets of carefully folded paper.

What you need:

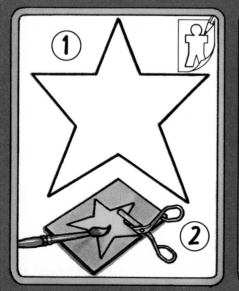
①
②

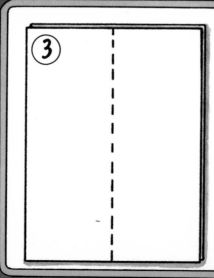
③

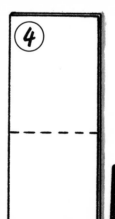
④

⑤

⑥

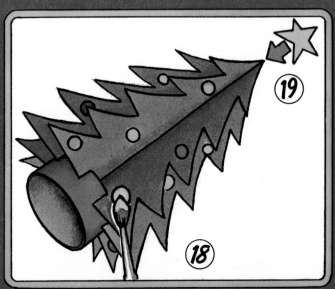

Lamb

- Used matchsticks are ideal for the legs but toothpicks can be used instead.

- Use any bottle top of suitable size – one from a toothpaste tube is perfect.

- Make the tail from a pipe cleaner or roll a piece of cotton between your fingers to make a tail shape and glue it into position.

What you need:

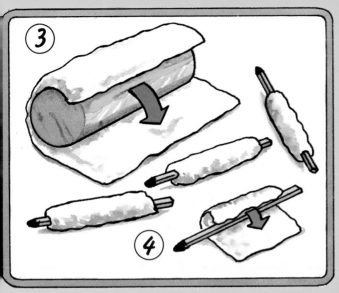

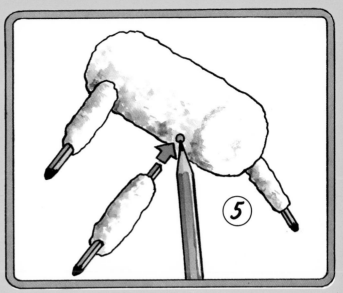

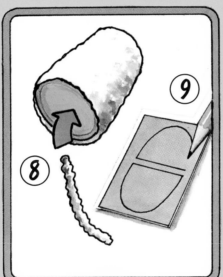

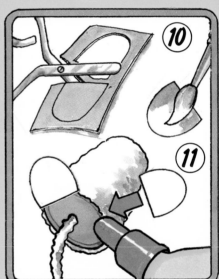

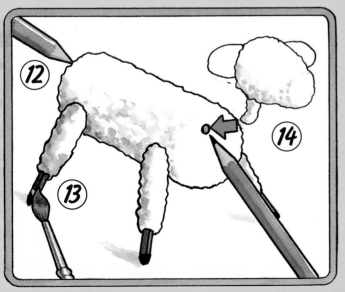

Donkey

- Trace the outline of the body, legs, and ears in picture 1 onto cardboard and cut out. The solid lines show where to cut and dotted lines show where to fold.

- Secure the string tail into position with modeling clay. The modeling clay is needed to balance the donkey.

What you need:

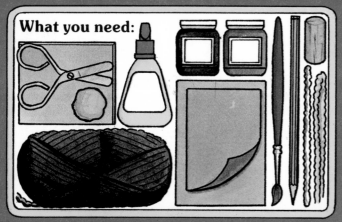

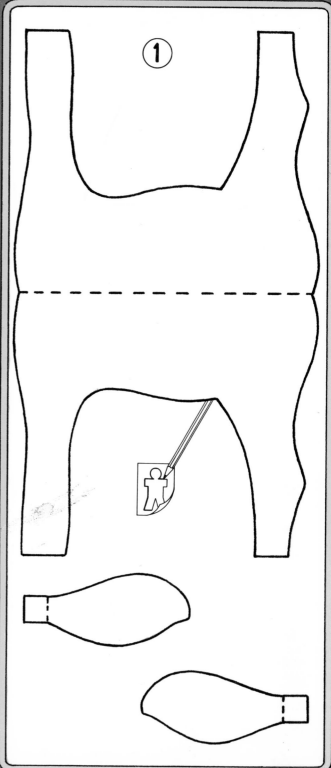

①

22

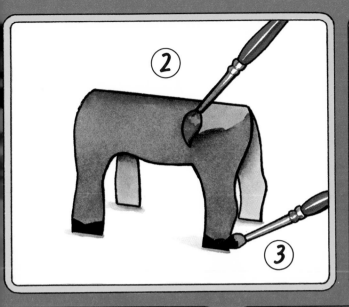

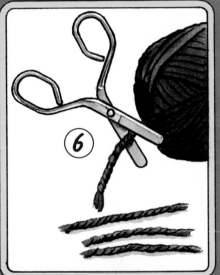

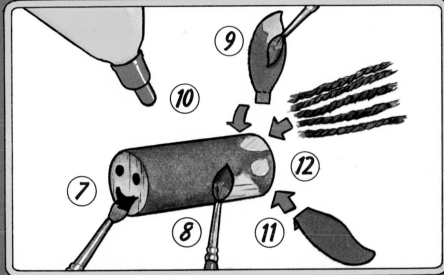

Cone People

- Use this model to make the people for the nativity scene.

- Trace the outline in picture 6 onto cardboard to make the arms.

- Draw around a dinner plate to make a cone of the correct size.

- Decorate the models with scraps of cloth, paint, or colored paper. See page 26.

What you need:

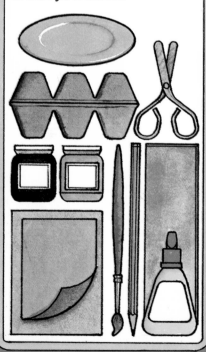

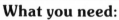

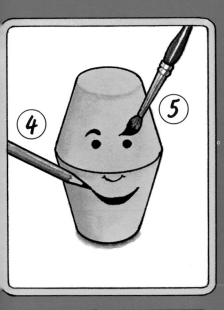

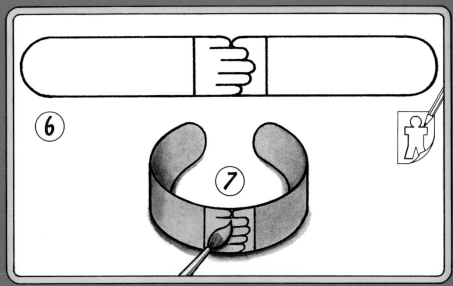

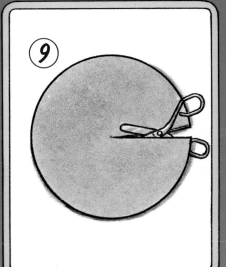

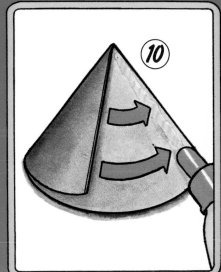

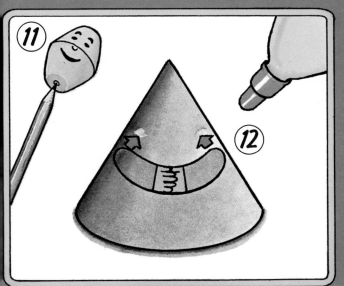

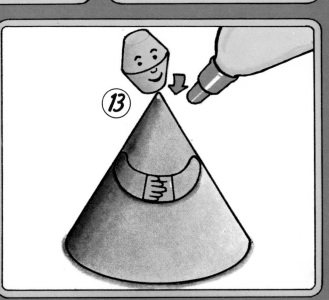

25

Mary and Joseph

- When you have made the models (see page 24), clothe and decorate them.

- Paint the cone bodies in different colors and stick on shapes from tin-foil or paper lace doilies.

- Paint yellow circles of card as haloes for Mary and Joseph.

- Use any scraps of cloth for the cloaks.

- Use knitting yarn or cotton for hair and beards.

What you need:

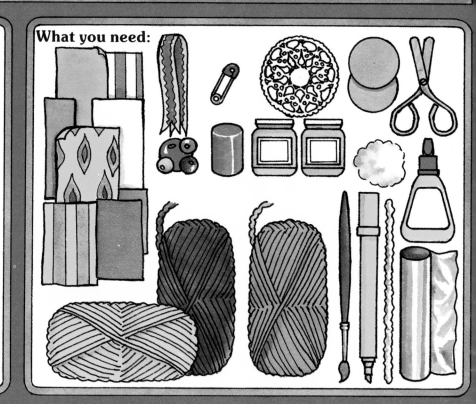

①

②

Shepherd and Three Kings

3

4

5

6

The Stable

- A very large cardboard box is needed for the stable. Cover the floor with straw or yellow yarn.

- If you do not have a bead to make Jesus' head, roll a ball of modeling clay to shape instead and paint it.

- A matchbox tray is ideal for the manger, but any box of similar size will work.

- Arrange your models in and around the stable to make a nativity scene.

What you need:

Jesus and Manger

Bits Box

Collect all sorts of household bits and pieces on a regular basis. Children can use them not only for making the projects in this book, but also for inventing models of their own. Here are a few suggestions, but anything at all may prove useful with a bit of imagination. Keep everything together in a "bits box."

Projects conceived by Vanessa Morgan
Art Editor Malcolm Smythe

30

PRINTED IN BELGIUM BY

INTERNATIONAL BOOK PRODUCTION

C

WITHDRAWN